The Dogtown Guide

Exploring an Abandoned Colonial Settlement on Cape Ann, Massachusetts

Mark J. Carlotto

The Dogtown Guide

Copyright © 2007 by Mark J. Carlotto

All rights reserved. No part of this book may be reproduced or transmitted in any form or by any means without written permission of the author.

ISBN: 978-0-557-00111-8

The author shall not be held responsible for any damage, loss, or liability, whether direct, indirect, or consequential, which arises or may arise from the use of this guide or any of the maps herein by any person or entity.

10 9 8 7 6 5 4 3 2 1

Foreword

Dogtown is a wondrous place. With its ancient stone walls and cellar holes, its glacial erratics—enormous boulders that seem to have been moved hundreds of feet by gigantic hands—its mix of old fields and meadows, forests, and sphagnum bogs, one could scarcely imagine its presence in the dead center of populous Cape Ann. Indeed, many otherwise interested visitors to these shores never learn about its existence; and there are residents, natives among them, who have scarcely set foot on any of the numerous trails Mark Carlotto walks us over in his compact new guide to Dogtown, a small wonder itself and a valuable addition to the growing body of resources about this stunningly beautiful island we all inhabit.

Concentrating the information from previous maps, guides and histories of Dogtown into less than a hundred pages is a feat in itself. But when one adds Carlotto's own experience of Dogtown gained from years of walking each trail, exploring the cellar holes, locating for himself the disappearing evidence of human habitation and use of the land, one possesses in this guide its most significant dimension: the author's own stamp, his feet on the ground experience of a place that is as formidable as it is mysterious.

Carlotto demystifies Dogtown in this concise guide, which we can carry with us, literally in the palm of one hand, on our own exploration of one of America's most intriguing abandoned settlements. The guide contains its own clear maps, each a section of a larger map that Carlotto has created from aerial photographs, topographical charts, existing trail maps, and his own meticulous walking over every inch of the terrain of Dogtown he describes in this superb guide.

Henry David Thoreau, who himself hiked across Dogtown in September of 1858, once said that "everywhere we go on the earth someone has been there before us." What Carlotto's guide helps us not only to see but to experience first hand is that Dogtown is both nature's creation and the work of human beings, who once built houses here, farming and grazing its cleared fields, logging its forests, and traveling by foot and ox cart over numerous roads, which connected the disparate parishes of Cape Ann from its earliest settlement until the 19th century.

Thoreau also wrote that "in wilderness is the preservation of the world." As we lead ever more hectic lives, finding less time for contemplation or solitude, we are going to need wild places like Dogtown, places where we can escape our over-mediated lives to walk among silent junipers and speechless boulders, listening again to our own thoughts while marveling once again at nature's handiwork. For this reason those of us who live on Cape Ann are fortunate to have Dogtown so close at hand and to be able to share its wonders with visitors. We can only be thankful that previous generations have valued Dogtown and worked to save and preserve it for posterity. And now we possess an important new key to Dogtown in this guide, which makes this great resource more accessible and understandable and therefore more immediate.

- Peter Anastas
  Former Chair, Dogtown Advisory Committee

Preface

The places we inhabit have their origins in the past. Cities were towns, and towns, villages. Before shopping malls were fields and farmland. There is a connection back in time to the first settlements, and beyond.

But there are places that are different, that had no future. Places that were abandoned, and eventually forgotten. Dogtown is one such place, which I learned about only after I had moved to Gloucester. As it turned out, the edge of Dogtown was in my very own backyard.

Looking out into the woods at night, I wondered what was out there. I read about the old settlement in the middle of Cape Ann, how it grew, and then declined after the Revolutionary War, and how the land, once forested, was cleared for its lumber. I learned that the land I now lived on was once part of a farm, whose animals would graze up in the pastures of Dogtown. After the cows had come home for the last time, trees and brush began to grow back. Deserted now for almost two hundred years, the houses were gone. Only their cellar holes remained. Camouflaged among the rocks and engulfed by vegetation, the vestiges of this former settlement were disappearing.

I spent hours and hours exploring Dogtown, walking along old roads and trails, following stonewalls into the woods. Stumbling across my first cellar hole, I wondered who had lived there, and what they had done for a living. The more I hiked in woods, the more I fell in love with Dogtown.

My background is in satellite imaging and remote sensing. Obtaining aerial photographs to see Dogtown from above, I was fascinated by what I saw:

Radiating out from the trails were stonewalls, some almost a mile in length, and other features not visible on the ground. Hiking through the brush I began to find structures in the middle of the Cape that no one had ever mentioned.

Exploring Dogtown on foot, I correlated what I found on the ground with aerial images and maps. Plotting the old roads and trails, locations of cellar holes, and other features in the area, a comprehensive picture began to take shape. I could see the original settlement, and how changes over time had transformed the landscape.

Combining collected information with historical sources, this book attempts to bridge a gap between existing field guides, maps, and narratives. Intended both as a reference and a guide for further exploration and discovery, *The Dogtown Guide* is written for those who already know about this deserted village in the middle of Cape Ann, as well as for visitors to Cape Ann who hear about Dogtown for the first time and want to experience this unique place for themselves.

Acknowledgements

A number of people have helped make this book possible. In particular, I thank Greg Gibson for introducing me to the woods of Dogtown, and Herb Stillman for sharing his extensive knowledge of Cape Ann's terrain and historical features. Thanks especially to my wife, Eileen, who, more than anyone, is the reason why I live here on this amazing island. The Dogtown Steering Committee, headed by Peter Anastas, suggested the need for a concise guide over twenty years ago. I hope this book fulfills that need and will lead to a greater appreciation of what we are fortunate to have here on Cape Ann.

Table of Contents

Introduction 1
   Organization of the Guide 2

Goose Cove Reservoir 7
   Common Road 13
   Adams Pines Trail 19

Dogtown Road 23
   Wharf Road 27
   Moraine Trail 27

Old Rockport Road 31
   Gloucester's First Mill 33
   Babson Boulder Trail and Old Gravel Road 37

Babson Shop 41
   Tarr Trail 45
   Luce Trail 47
   Art's and Nellie's Trails 53

Rockport Town Forest Trail 55

Interior of the Commons 59

Appendix 65
   Geographic Coordinates of Cellar Holes and Other Sites in Dogtown 67
   Roger Babson 69

Bibliography 71

Index 73

Introduction

> Not all who wander are lost. – *J.R.R. Tolkien*

Twenty miles north of Boston, in the middle of Cape Ann, lies an abandoned colonial settlement. At the tip of Cape Ann is Gloucester – America's oldest seaport. Today, much of the population lives less than a mile from the coast. Yet, at one time, there was a small village in the middle of the Cape. Half a century after the town of Gloucester was first settled, people began to live in the Commons Settlement, named for the thousand or so acres of common woodland out of which it grew. At its peak, more than forty families lived in this part of town. Then, around the time of the Revolutionary War, the village began to decline as commercial interests shifted from logging and agriculture to fishing and trading, and people moved to be closer to the harbor. By the early 1800's, the area, which had become known as Dogtown, was a ghost town.

Cold and lonely in the winter, some have compared the middle of the Cape to the Scottish Moors; others imagine the enormous boulders strewn all over the bleak landscape as strange megalithic monuments of earlier times. Yet, scattered here and there are telltale signs of prior habitation: stonewalls, a familiar sight in New England, old roads and trails, and cellar holes – the only visible remains of the village that was once here.

Walking along the old roads and trails, one wonders how anyone could have lived in such a place.

Overgrown with vegetation it is difficult to picture the old settlement. It is hard to understand why some of the early settlers lived here, and how they survived.

Dogtown can be inscrutable. Without a map, it is easy to get lost in the network of old roads and trails that crisscross the interior of the Cape. Even with a map, many of its secrets remain hidden behind thick brush and cat briar.

History books have little to say about Dogtown, other than to speculate on its decline and eventual desertion almost two centuries ago. For those interested in learning about Dogtown, the best way is on foot. *The Dogtown Guide* leads the reader and explorer through what is left of the old settlement by relating the history of Dogtown and its inhabitants to the current landscape.

Organization of the Guide

Dogtown offers a variety of terrain for hiking, biking, rock-climbing, cross-country skiing, and other kinds of recreational activities. Although the roads are wider, some can be rocky in places. Trails range from leisurely footpaths through hardscrabble and woods to narrow winding paths through boulder fields.

This guide covers the area bounded by Squam Road to the north, the Town of Rockport trails to the east, Old Rockport Road to the south, and Goose Cove Reservoir to the west. Trails around Loop Pond in Rockport, discussed in Helen Naismith's book, *Walking Cape Ann*, are not covered here. Also not covered are the trails north of Squam Road towards Lanesville and west to Dennison Street as there is no direct public access (with parking) to these trails except via those from the south.

There are five convenient places to enter Dogtown (Figure 1):

Goose Cove Reservoir (1) provides good overall access to the western part of Dogtown. To get there, take Route 128 north over the Annisquam River into Gloucester. Go north on Washington Street at the first traffic circle (three quarters of the way around) just over the bridge. After about a mile bear right onto Gee Avenue (look for the sign to the Beeman School) and follow it to the parking lot at the end of the street.

Dogtown Common (2) is best for a quick visit to Dogtown Road and a few, easy to find, cellar holes along the way. Follow the above directions. Before reaching the parking lot at the end of Gee Avenue, take a right onto Cherry Street. Look for the entrance to Dogtown Common on the left. Follow the road up the hill to the parking lot at the end. A gate blocks vehicular traffic past this point.

Old Rockport Road (3) is close to a number of Roger Babson's inscribed boulders on the south side of the Babson Reservoir. It is a steep climb down and across the reservoir to get to the others. To get there, take Route 128 to the second traffic circle, and go three quarters of the way around it into Blackburn Industrial Park. The entrance to the old road is on the left, across from the National Oceanographic and Atmospheric Administration (NOAA) building.

The James Babson Shop (4) is the best way to get to Dogtown from the Rockport side of the Cape. Take Route 128 all the way to the end, make a left at the traffic light onto Eastern Avenue. About a half a mile past Calvary Cemetery, look for the Babson Shop at Beaver Dam on the left.

For those interested in different terrain and habitats, the Rockport Town Forest Trail (5) is close to Briar Swamp and trails to the north that lead to Cape Ann's quarries. One can park at the Rockport train station. Walk into Evans Field and look for granite steps going up a hill on the left side of the field. This path leads to the Town Forest Trail and Squam Path.

The first five sections of the guide discuss the trails in these areas, and what one can expect to see along each. The last section explores the interior of Dogtown Commons. Up is north in all maps[1]. The scale of the trail maps is 1:9600, or about 800 feet per inch, and 1:27,600 for the overview map in Figure 1.

An appendix gives the geographical locations of cellar holes, Babson's Boulders, and other features of interest. This information can be loaded into a handheld GPS[2] and used to navigate to these locations in Dogtown. Cellar holes are labeled according to Roger Babson's numbering scheme, proceeded by a 'C'. B1-B26 refers to the Babson Boulders. L1-L4 identifies several other points of

---

[1] A scanned 1:25,000 scale USGS topographic map provides the geographic base. Aerial imagery was downloaded from the State of Massachusetts web site (www.mass.gov/mgis) and registered to the base map.

[2] The global positioning system (GPS) is a constellation of satellites developed and maintained by the U.S. Air Force. Similar to those found in cars, a handheld GPS receiver can be used to determine the location of a receiver anywhere on earth where there is satellite coverage.

interest in the middle of the Cape. A list of references is provided at the end for those interested in learning more about Cape Ann and Dogtown.

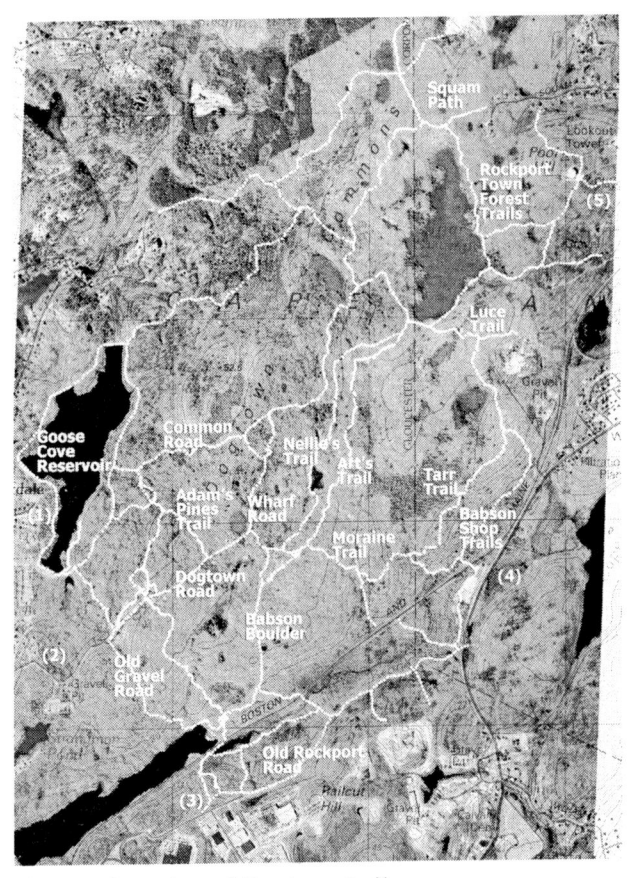

Figure 1 Overview of Dogtown trails.

Figure 2 Goose Cove Reservoir

Goose Cove Reservoir

The parking area at the end of Gee Avenue, at the entrance to Goose Cove Reservoir, is an excellent place to enter Dogtown (at the arrow in Figure 2). After passing through the gate, one comes to an asphalt service road that encircles the reservoir.

Heading north (left) on the service road leads to the first of four dams and dikes that were constructed in the early 1960s to form the reservoir. A footpath off the main service road takes us over the southwest dike, which provides a panoramic view of the reservoir. Seagulls, cormorants, and other birds are frequent visitors. Merging with the service road on the other side of the dike, we enter a stretch of forest. Glacial boulders are all around. Continuing along, we cross over the northwest dike. After another brief interlude in the woods, we reach the north dam. Looking to the right, the south end of the reservoir is about 2/3 mile away. To the left, a steep valley leads down to Dennison Street.

On the other side of the north dam, a trail leading to Whale's Jaw branches off and goes up and over the hill front of us. A side trail off of this leads to an old stone foundation with a fireplace (S6) offering a seasonal view of the reservoir looking south. This site post-dates the original Commons Settlement.

Continuing along on the east side of the reservoir we begin to notice stonewalls leading into the woods. These were once common woodlands. Land grants in 1688 gave each resident of Gloucester their own six-acre lot, plus use of these woodlands. Crossing a happy brook trickling down from high wetlands to the east, more stonewalls can be seen, beckoning us to follow.

Figure 3 Large boulder marking location of Cellar 29. Site 30 is behind the photographer.

Soon we arrive at the intersection of Common Road. Flooding the valley to our right, split Gee Avenue (formerly Common Road) in two. Back at the entrance on the other side of the reservoir, if you walk across the service road and down to the water, one of Roger Babson's inscriptions (29) can be seen on a huge boulder marking the location of the home of William Hilton, which was later occupied by John Morgan Stanwood, also known as Granther Stannard (Figure 3). The old road ran south of this cellar and past another (C30) now under water. According to Babson, there were two houses there, which belonged to Joshua Hunter and Joshua Elwell. One of them was once a cobbler shop. Continuing on to the northeast the old road crossed a brook that ran through the middle of the valley, past the place where we are now standing, and continued up the hill to our left. A few sections of stonewall that had flanked the old road can be found off in the brush to our right.

Figure 4 Boulder next to site 29 at the high water mark

Continuing on, now about two-thirds around the reservoir, the road climbs to its highest point. To the left a footpath branches off to a scenic overlook (L3) with views of the reservoir and Ipswich Bay. Originally forested, the middle of the Cape was extensively lumbered by the late 1600's. The Annisquam (formerly known as the Squam) River and Ipswich Bay could be seen from much of the interior of the Cape. With the return of the forest, this is one of the few places left in Dogtown that offer a water view.

As rapidly as it had ascended, the service road descends as we approach the south end of the reservoir. A trail on the left just before the dam leads to Dogtown Road. A good way to get to Dogtown Road from the Goose Cove Reservoir parking lot is to walk the other way around the reservoir. Past the south dam just ahead, make a right onto this trail. The trail leads up a hill past a scenic view of a pond to the right. Walking over a concrete retaining wall, through old stonewalls, and crossing a brook, we come to Dogtown Road. A cellar hole (C9) is on the left just past a gate (see Figure 14).

Returning to the reservoir service road and the south dam, a trail can be found just before the dam, which runs back along the east shore of the reservoir. When the water level is low enough one can follow it down to a stonewall that parallels the shoreline. Before the reservoir was built, this land had been a meadow.

Continuing past the south dam, another third of a mile or so takes us around the reservoir and back to where we started. On the way out, just before the parking lot on the left, hidden by brush, is another one of Babson's inscriptions (28) with the cellar hole behind it. According to Babson, this was the Bennett farm. Local residents remember the time before the reservoir was built when cows would graze up in Dogtown, returning at night to farms along Gee Avenue.

Figure 5 Dam at the south end of Goose Cove Reservoir

If you have the time, walk down Gee Avenue and look for an inscribed "27" on the left side of the street partially buried under the pavement. Here stood the "Castle." The original house was built by Anthony Bennett in 1679, and was one of the first houses in this part of town. It is the only remaining house of the original settlement.

Further on at the corner of Stanwood and Gee Avenue is the number "26" engraved on a large rock, marking the Stanwood House, and the western-most point of Dogtown.

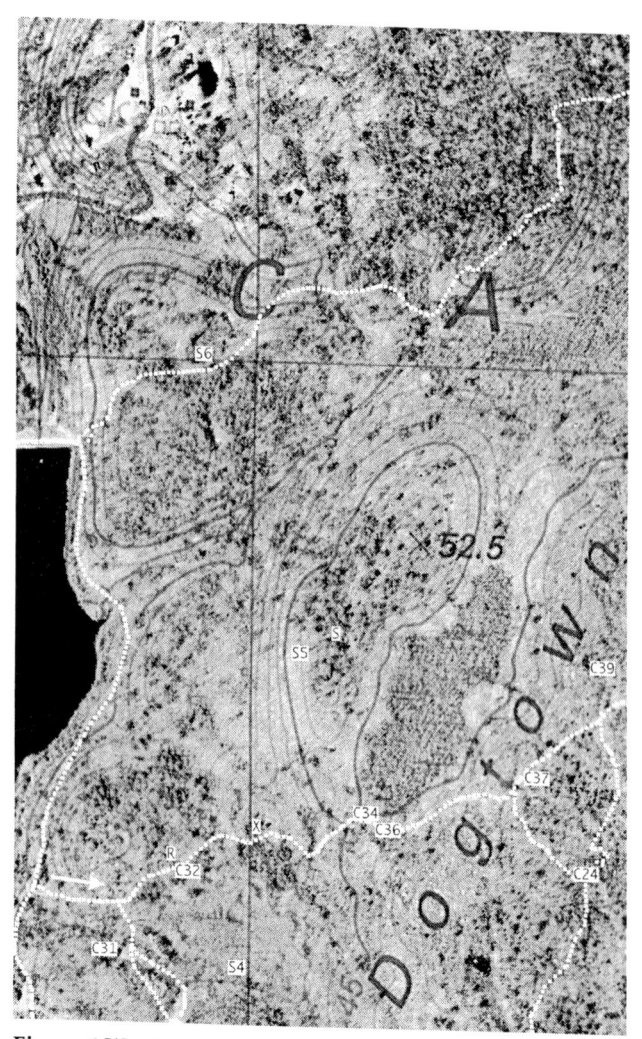

Figure 6 Western section of Common Road

Common Road

As noted in the previous section, before Goose Cove Reservoir was created, Common Road (now Gee Avenue) ran from Washington Street, past Peter's Pulpit, up to Whale's Jaw. Today, it begins at the service road on the east side of the reservoir (at the arrow in Figure 6).

Walking up the hill, notice the stonewalls on either side of the road. The walls kept cows and other animals that were being lead along the road on the road and off private property. At the top of the hill, the Adams Pines Trail branches off to the right. A short distance further on, just behind the wall on the left, is a cellar (R) covered by vines and bushes. This is where Judy Rhines and Liz Tucker lived. These two women were among Dogtown's more colorful residents. Across the road is cellar 32.

Farther up on the left is another cellar hole (X), also under thick brush. The cellars on the north side of Common Road border a sea of cat briar and bittersweet. If you can get past the thicket, there is a small stream that parallels the road. A little stone footbridge crosses the stream. According to Babson, a trail branched off Common Road at around this point and headed up the hill to the north.

On top of this hill is a site (S) that was originally the home of Nehemiah Stanwood. According to Charles E. Mann in his *Story of Dogtown*, this site was later occupied by Peter Lurvey, a hero of the American Revolution, and others, the last being Cornelius Finson ("Black Neil"). Finson was Dogtown's last inhabitant, dying in the winter of 1839. Local legend is that he lived in the cellar under the floorboards guarding Captain Kidd's treasure.

Continuing east on Common Road, we pass two more cellars (C34) and (C36) on either side of the road. To the left is what used to be the Beech Pasture, a part of the thousand or so acres of common pasture land used by the early settlers. Over the years, it has become so overgrown that it is almost impossible to penetrate on foot. Farther along, we come to another cellar hole on the right (C37) just past a short cut over to Wharf Road. Copeland and Rogers tell us in *The Saga of Cape Ann* that a blacksmith shop was located in this area. At the intersection with Wharf Road, the stonewall on the left veers into the woods. Following it in leads to the site of Benjamin Allen's home (C39).

Figure 7 Beech Pasture on Common Road

Continuing on Common Road (Figure 9), we pass a an unmarked cellar hole. Then in front of us looms Peter's Pulpit (L2). This enormous rock, like the other boulders around us, is called an erratic, having been carried hundreds of miles by the glaciers that once covered this part of North America. Looking around, we are surrounded by trees. Yet, less than a century ago, this had been open space, a vast pastureland that extended west all the way to the Mill River.

Figure 8 Whale's Jaw

We are at the extreme eastern edge of the original Commons Settlement. At this point Common Road heads north. The Luce Trail joins us about a half a mile north of Peter's Pulpit. Going left over a brook we soon reach another famous erratic, Whale's Jaw (L1). When Whale's Jaw was first discovered hundreds of years ago, the rock was split in two, resembling the open jaws of a whale. Then in 1989, someone lit a fire under it, causing the "jaw" to crack and collapse. Like New Hampshire's Old Man of the Mountain, which fell in 2003, the illusion is gone. Still, it is a powerful spot and worth the visit.

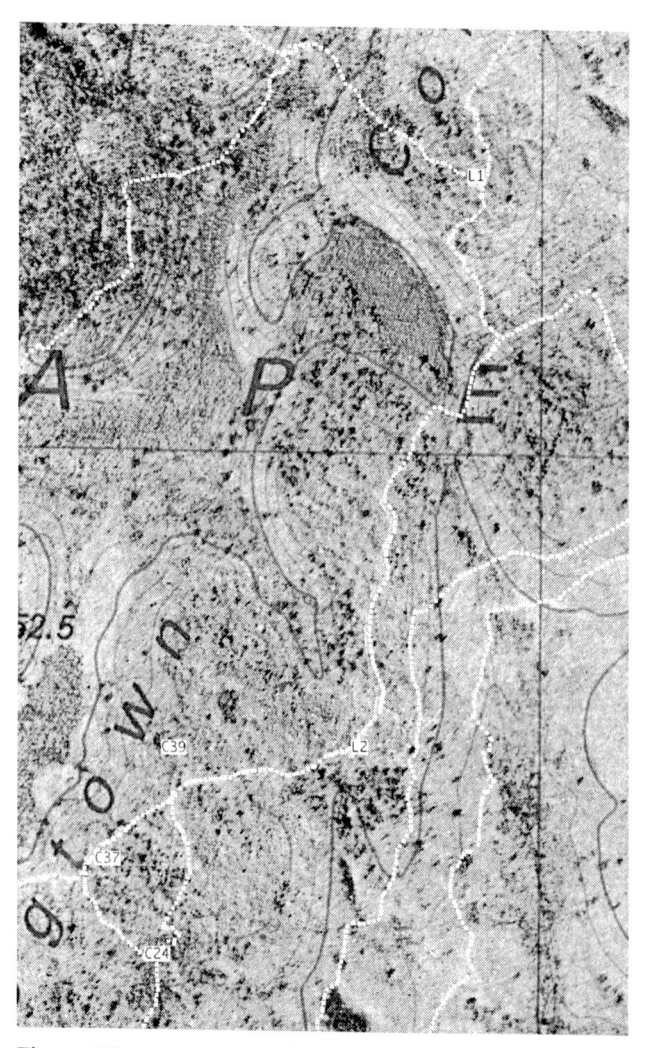

Figure 9 Eastern section of Common Road

We are now on the Luce Trail, heading north to the Squam Path and Lanesville. For those who wish to return to Goose Cove Reservoir, an alternative to backtracking is to follow a trail that heads west from here and leads to the north dam (Figure 9). Turning left, the trail goes behind Whale's Jaw. A quarter of a mile in, it crosses a stream. It is easy to lose our way at this point. If we continue straight, a path will take us to the Dennison Trail and the upper end of Dennison Street. Instead, look to the left for a trail that hugs the stream. This trail ascends into a pine forest and follows the high road above the wetlands area north of the Commons. At one point, near the top of a hill, we pass through a stonewall.

Figure 10 Stone foundation and fireplace. Goose Cove Reservoir is in the background.

Less than a quarter of a mile away from the reservoir, we descend and meet up with a dirt road. This road

17

leads to Dennison Street. Instead of following the road, look for a trail branching off and leading up a hill to the left. Taking this path leads us west toward the reservoir. Nearing the end of our trek, an old stone foundation and fireplace (S6) can be seen to the right just before descending to the service road at the north dam (Figure 2).

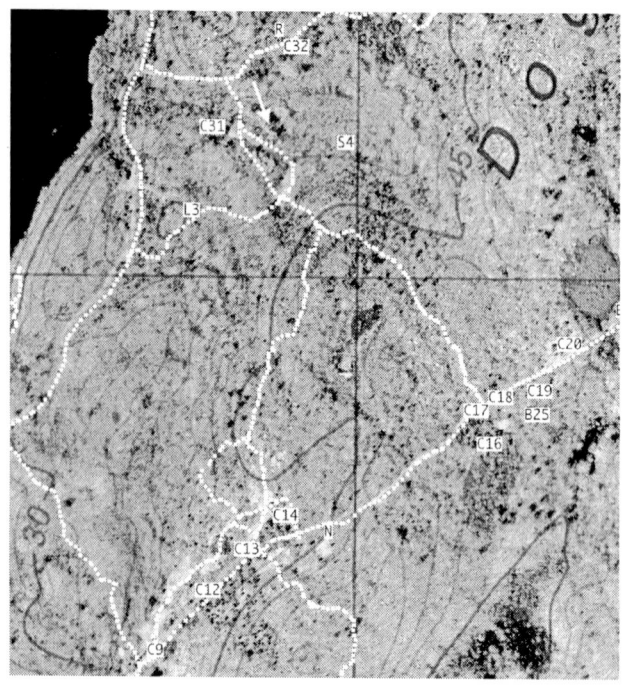

Figure 11 Adams Pines Trail

Adams Pines Trail

The Adams Pines Trail (known as the Cross Dogtown Trail in some maps) runs between Common Road and Dogtown Road. Starting from Common Road (at arrow in Figure 11), a commemorative stone can be found in the brush off to the right, just before a brook. Past the brook on the right is a cellar (C31). The two are related. From the July 18, 1932 edition of *Time* magazine:

"On the boulders of Dogtown Common, part of Cape Ann near Gloucester, Mass., lately appeared carved legends such as "Prosperity Follows Service," "Be Clean," "Help Mother," "Get a Job," "Save." When one such marking, the simple number "31," was carved on a boulder on the property of Mrs. Leila Webster Adams, widow of Manhattan architect Rayne Adams and descendant of early settlers, she rose up in protest, revealed the carver to be Roger Ward Babson, famed statistician. Explained Statistician Babson, whose family settled on Cape Ann in 1628: "The work I'm doing is part of an educational plan... which will take me some years to complete... In short, I believe young people when outdoors should see something besides advertisements to smoke certain brands of cigarets and to use certain soaps to return that schoolgirl complexion."

Back to the trail, we have two choices. Either way leads to the region in Dogtown known as Adam's Pines (Figure 12). Going left, we reach a clearing. Off to the far left, overlooking wetlands to the east, is a stone foundation (S4). The foundation is made of granite cut from one of Cape Ann's quarries. Going right at the split takes us past several old lots separated by stonewalls, meeting back up with the first trail at the clearing.

Figure 12 Adams Pines was once a tree farm

At this point, we are faced with another decision. The path to the right, under a phalanx of pines, leads through a stonewall and up a hill to the overlook (L3) on the east side of Goose Cove Reservoir. Going straight takes us through a cathedral of pines, up a hill, and on to Dogtown Road, emerging between cellars C17 and C18. In between, we can visit a vernal pond off on the right, which is visible through the trees in winter. A less traveled path branches off to the right near the top of the hill in front of us. This trail follows an old stonewall south. Nearing Dogtown Road, it splits into several footpaths as the woods thin to heath. We find ourselves in what was the Winslow farm, now a sparsely vegetated area behind cellar holes C9-C14, at the south end of Dogtown Road.

Figure 13 View of Ipswich Bay from overlook off Goose Cove Reservoir service road

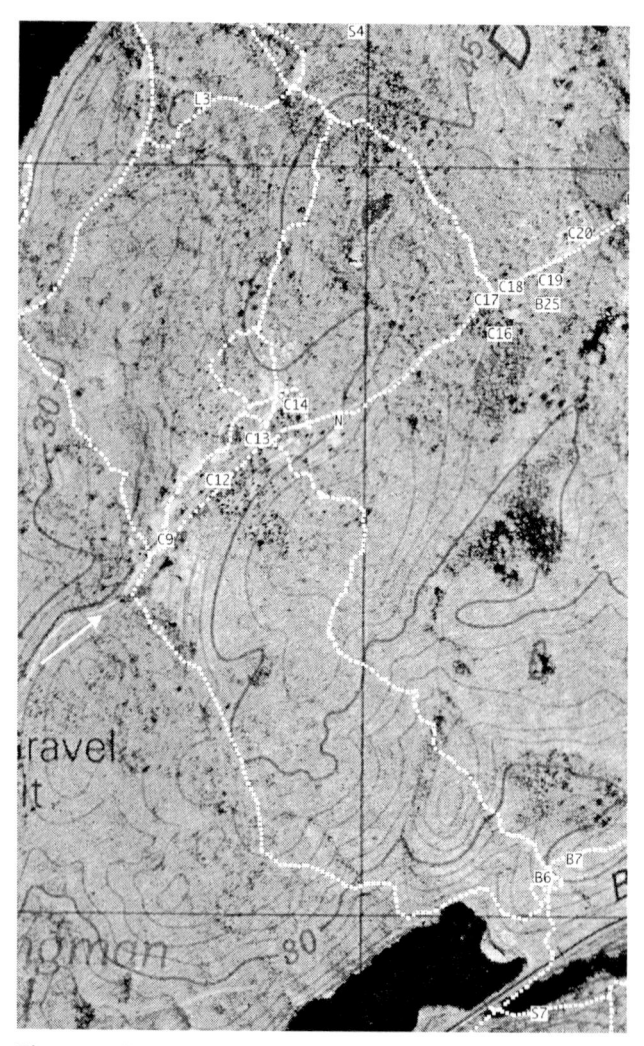

Figure 14 Dogtown Road to Granny Day's Swamp

Dogtown Road

The sign "Dogtown Common" on Cherry Street marks the start of Dogtown Road. A gate at the parking lot blocks vehicular traffic. Walking past it, we pass Old Gravel Road on the right, which leads down to the Babson Reservoir. (This is the first trail on the right just past the arrow in Figure 14.) Just before a second gate up ahead is a trail off to the left to Goose Cove Reservoir. On the other side of the gate is a cellar hole (9) on the left. Cellars 9, 12, and 13 are close to the road; cellar 14 is farther off to the left, hidden behind trees and brush. This area was once a farm that belonged to Joseph Winslow. All of these cellars are marked by Babson's inscriptions on nearby boulders[3]. In addition, several other unmarked cellars can be found along this stretch of road.

Just past cellar 14 on the right is a knoll where Easter Carter's house, the only two-story house in Dogtown, used to be. It was a popular gathering place in the early 1800's where local residents would come for a boiled cabbage dinner. A sand pit is all that remains of the site. The stone marker (15) has been moved to the other side of the road. Just past it, beyond a stonewall, is another cellar hole (N).

Continuing up a gradual incline through an unpopulated section of the rocky road, we come to a

---

[3] Cellars 1-8 along Cherry Street and the lower end of Dogtown Road no longer exist. For more information see Roger Babson's *Cape Ann Tourists Guide*.

cluster of cellar holes. C17 and C18 are on the left, on either side of the junction with the Adams Pines Trail. C16 and C19 are harder to find, off the road to the right. This is the high point on Dogtown Road, about 180 feet above sea level.

Figure 15 Dogtown Road between Cellars N and 16

Just past C18, a little footpath branches off to the right. On the left are two stones marking the death of James Merry, who was killed while fighting a bull in 1892 (Figure 16). The pasture on the right is where it happened. The incident was immortalized by Charles Olson in his epic poem, "Maximus, From Dogtown – I." At the end of the footpath is a boulder with the inscription: "Never Try Never Win." This is one of numerous boulders scattered throughout Dogtown that were carved by unemployed stonecutters under the direction of Roger Babson in the 1930's.

Back on Dogtown Road, a bit further along on the left is the site of a small schoolhouse (C20) run by Jane "Granny" Day in the early days of the settlement[4]. It is on a small hill surrounded by pine trees. The area around the site is sparsely vegetated with clumps of trees and bushes here and there. Faint footpaths seem to lead everywhere, but go nowhere.

Figure 16 Stone where James Merry was first attacked

---

[4] Before 1725 private schools for small children existed in the more thickly settled parts of the Cape. In 1735 Gloucester was divided into seven school districts. Each district provided a schoolhouse that was used on a part-time, or circulating, basis for classes. One was located in the part of town that included the Commons Settlement. Whether Granny Day's schoolhouse belonged to the school district, or was one of the private schools, is not known.

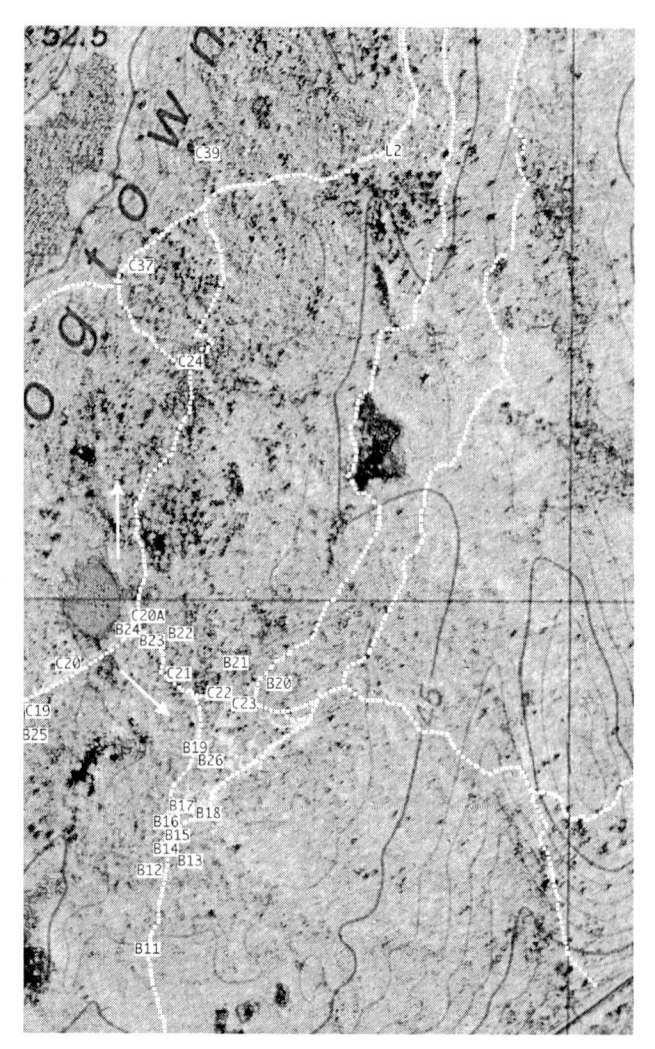

Figure 17 Wharf Road and Moraine Trail

Wharf Road

On the other side of Granny Day's Swamp (Figure 17), at the Dogtown Square (DTSQ) marker on the right, the road splits. To the left is Wharf Road (up arrow). Surrounded by rocks and boulders, there is a filled-in well and cellar hole (C20a) near the beginning on the right. According to Irving Sucholeiki, who excavated an area around the cellar, this was probably the site of Granny Day's home in the mid 1700's.

Continuing north on Wharf Road, we pass a vernal pool off to the left. About a quarter of a mile up from DTSQ, just past a small trail on the left, is a well to the right. This is perhaps the "darkest" place in all of Dogtown. Beyond Babson's marker (24), surrounded by trees and brush, is the cellar of Abraham Wharf, who committed suicide in the winter of 1814. Quickening our pace, we soon reach Common Road near Benjamin Allen's cellar (C39).

Moraine Trail

Back at DTSQ, going right at the split[5] (down arrow) puts us on the Moraine Trail, which leads to the south side of Dogtown. The north end of the trail is marked by the inscription "Moraine" on a small rock on the left. The first quarter of a mile or so is very

---

[5] In Copeland and Rogers *The Saga of Cape Ann* this is called "the parting path" that Charles E. Mann in his *Story of Dogtown* places near the home of James Witham, a sheep farmer in the early 1700's. This site (C21) was later occupied by James Robinson.

busy with a number of paths branching off on either side. To the left are cellar holes 21 and 22, and footpaths leading off into woods to several of Babson's larger boulders ("Keep Out of Debt," "If Work Stops Values Decay," and "Prosperity Follows Service").

Figure 18 Cellar hole (C22) along the Moraine Trail

The first two cellar holes are near the trail and easy to spot (Figure 18). Cellar 23 is off the trail to the right, obscured by dense brush and vines. Several other structures can be found nearby. This area was once a farm that belonged to Colonel William Pearce, who was one of the wealthiest men in Gloucester at the time. Just before this site, the Babson Boulder Trail branches off to the right. Just after it, another path splits off to Uncle Andrew's Rock, "Spiritual Power," by way of the Pearce Pasture. Often the second path is mistaken for the Moraine Trail, which is the less obvious trail to the left.

Figure 19 Old well near the Pearce cellar (C23)

Continuing on the Moraine Trail we pass Nellie's and Art's Trails on the left, both of which lead to the Briar Swamp. Our trail begins its descent through the terminal moraine at this point. After about a quarter of a mile, the Tarr Trail branches off to the left near a spring at marker[6] #11. As the Moraine Trail continues down its rocky course, it passes through a marshy area, which can be difficult to pass at certain times of the year. Finally, the trail reaches its terminus at the

---

[6] Trail markers were posted throughout Dogtown in the 1980's. For more information, see the *Dogtown Common Trail Map*, which is available in local bookstores.

railroad tracks. The Babson Shop is a third of a mile down the tracks to the left. Instead of walking this distance along the tracks, a safer option is to find an opening on the other side of the tracks a few hundred feet down on the right. This leads to a trail that parallels the tracks and ends up at the Babson Shop at Beaver Dam.

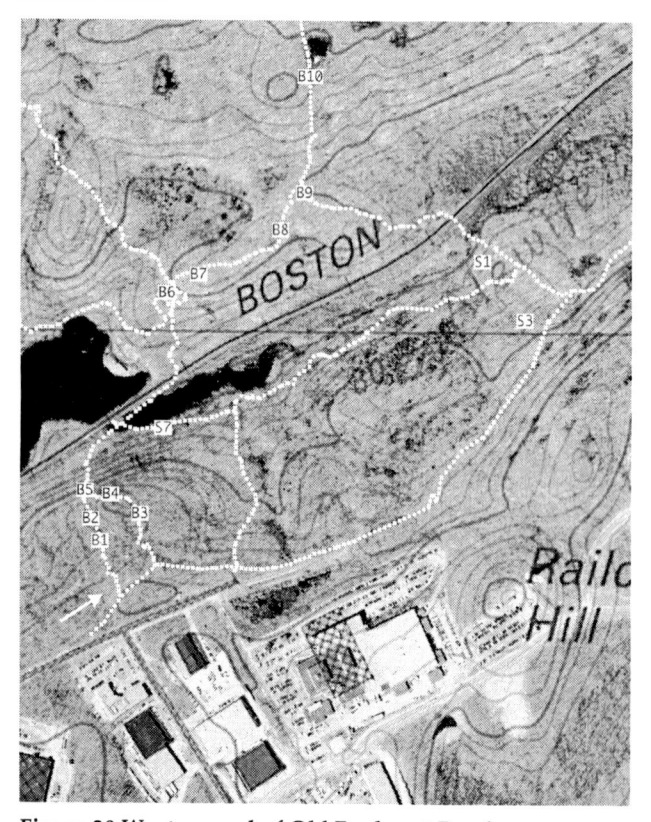

Figure 20 Western end of Old Rockport Road

Old Rockport Road

The Old Rockport Road appears in the oldest maps of Gloucester. In Mason's 1831 map of Gloucester and Cape Ann, it is called "Old Road from the Cape to Town Parish." Originally, it was the only road between Meeting House Green[7] and Sandy Bay (Rockport). One enters what is left of this road at a barrier across from the National Oceanographic and Atmospheric Administration (NOAA) building in the Blackburn Industrial Park (at the arrow in Figure 20.)

A short distance in, on the left, is the start of the Babson Boulder Trail at Tent Rock. Five (B1-B5) of the inscribed boulders are on this side of the railroad tracks ("Get a Job," "Help Mother," "Be True," "Be Clean," and "Save"), and so can be visited without much effort.

After a few hundred feet, another trail can be found on the left. This trail, which is an old ox cart route, descends to the eastern end of Babson Reservoir. Going left leads to an abandoned granite quarry (S7), along the railroad tracks. Going right follows Alewife Brook upstream to the site of Gloucester's first mill

---

[7] Gloucester, like other colonial towns, was divided into parishes. Each parish had a meetinghouse – a combination of today's church and town hall. The Commons Settlement was in Gloucester's First Parish, whose Meeting House and Green were located near where the first traffic circle (Grant Circle) is today.

(S1). This side trail offers a good view of the brook and the valley, particularly in winter.

About a half a mile farther along Old Rockport Road, look for a cellar hole (S3) on the left, just before the trail down to the old mill site. According to Roger Babson, this was a schoolhouse operated by James Babson's in-laws in the mid 1600's.

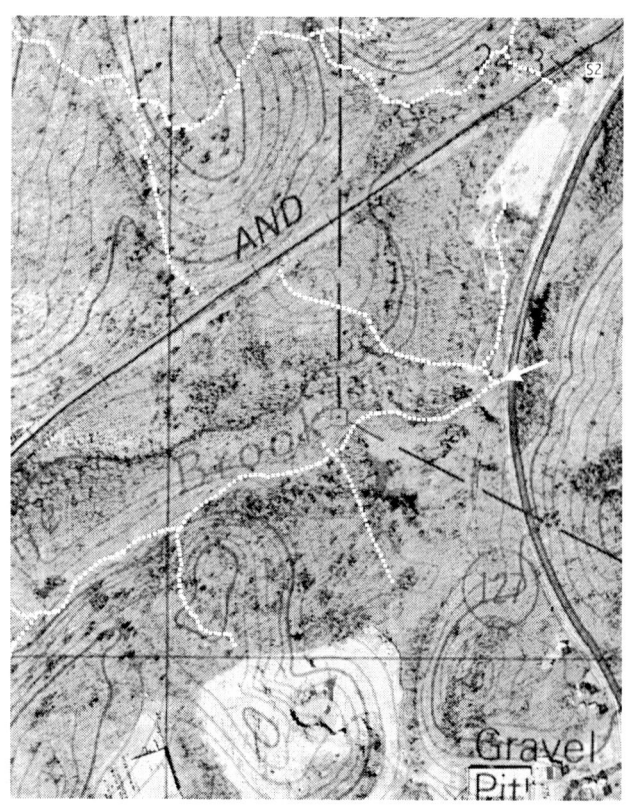

Figure 21 Eastern end of Old Rockport Road

Old Rockport Road continues on for another two thirds of a mile ending at a barrier on Eastern Avenue (at arrow in Figure 20). In between, several footpaths branch off on either side. A number of cellar holes can be found in this area. Just before Eastern Avenue, a path leads off to the left, passing through a stonewall. After a short distance, it splits in two. Following the left fork leads over Alewife Brook to an opening at the railroad tracks, not far from the Moraine Trail on the other side of the tracks. The right fork takes us on a leisurely stroll paralleling Eastern Avenue, ending in a meadow at the Babson Shop about a third of a mile away.

Figure 22 Babson's map of the old mill site over an aerial photograph

Gloucester's First Mill

Like Dogtown, there is very little in history books about Gloucester's first mill. The most informative source is Roger Babson's *Cape Ann Tourist's Guide*. According to Babson, a mill was built on Cape Pond

Brook (now Alewife Brook) in 1642. It was used as a sawmill for most of the year, and to grind corn in the fall. In those days, a significant amount of water flowed down the brook into the Mill River at Riverdale. According to Babson:

"An earthen dam about 170 feet long was built, the base 20 feet and the top 10 feet wide. It extended westward from a large rock on the east end, almost to what is now the railroad land on the west end. This dam was about 10 feet high and held back the waters into a millpond at the north. This covered about a half square mile of area and averaged some ten feet deep."

The dam was dismantled and the millpond drained in 1932 at the time the Babson Reservoir was created[8].

Evidence of the millpond can be seen in aerial photography; otherwise, very little else can be discerned from the air (Figure 22). With the help of Babson's map and narrative, one can still find traces of the mill site on the ground. The mill itself was located below the dam to the southwest (Figure 23). Facing downstream, look for a ditch on the left that parallels the brook. Water flowed down the ditch and over a water wheel that powered the mill. A rectilinear pattern of stones marks this spot. Uphill and to the left of the mill, there is a hollow. This is probably where sawed lumber was stacked before it was loaded onto ox carts for transport.

---

[8] Sometimes beavers build a dam across the brook where the old earthen dam used to be. This causes a large area upstream to become flooded.

The mill site can be reached from the south via Old Rockport Road. One can also get there from Dogtown by following a path that branches off from the Babson Boulder Trail at the boulder "To Rockport" (B9), descends a steep hill, and crosses over the railroad tracks just north of the site (Figure 24).

Figure 23 Site of Gloucester's first mill

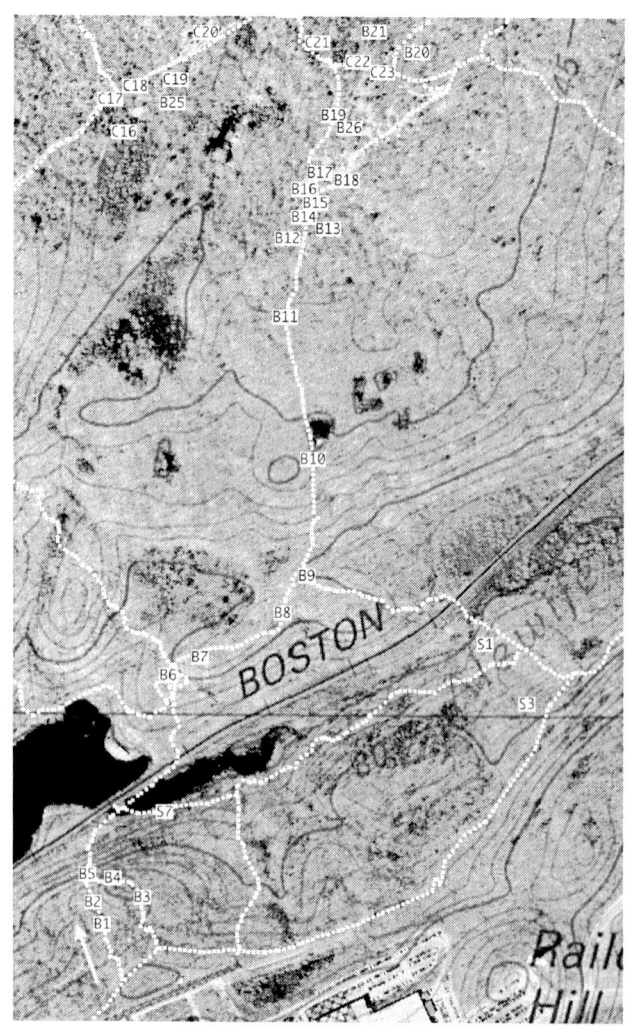

Figure 24 Babson Boulder Trail

Babson Boulder Trail and Old Gravel Road

The Babson Boulder Trail, originally called the Tent Rock Trail, starts near Tent Rock, just off Old Rockport Road (see arrow in Figure 24), runs north across the railroad tracks, around Babson Reservoir, and up to Dogtown Road. The first five Babson Boulders (B1-B5) are south of the reservoir. After passing "Save" (B5), the trail begins a steep descent down to the railroad tracks. At the tracks, go right for about five hundred feet. The trail reappears on the left and goes up a hill to the right of a sand pit at the east end of the reservoir.

At this point, we encounter several connecting trails. The first one to the left before "Truth" (B6), hugs the northern edge of the reservoir and leads up to the Old Gravel Road (Figure 14). This route can be difficult along the reservoir when the water level is high. Farther along, it crosses a stream, which drains the terrain south of Dogtown Road. This too can be a bit tricky, especially after heavy rain or snowmelt. Eventually the trail widens as it winds up the hill to Dogtown. A large boulder can be seen off to the right just before reaching Dogtown Road.

Back to the Babson Boulder Trail, after passing "Truth", another trail braches off to the left that also leads up to Dogtown Road. Crossing upstream from the previous trail, we climb though heavy glacial debris. Passing stonewalls in the middle of all this, one wonders why anyone would care about sub-dividing up such a place. There are enormous boulders everywhere, some bigger than Peter's Pulpit or Uncle Andrew's Rock. Just before reaching Dogtown Road, the path opens up at the top of a hill revealing a surprise view of Ipswich Bay in the distance. This path intersects Dogtown Road near cellar hole 14.

Figure 25 "Courage" is midway on the Babson Boulder Trail

Back again on the Boulder Trail, we pass "Work" (B7) "Courage" (B8) and "To Rockport" (B9). This is the junction of a trail that leads south back over the railroad tracks, past Gloucester's first mill, and on to the Old Rockport Road (Figure 26).

Returning to the main trail, the parade of boulders continues as we march north towards Dogtown. Passing a vernal pond to the right, the Babson Boulder Trail has literally become a trail of boulders. Some of the inscribed rocks are on the trail; others are more difficult to find, hidden in the woods along our route. About a third of a mile up from "To Rockport" we come to Uncle Andrew's Rock, "Spiritual Power"

(B18). This is the spiritual nexus of the Boulders, most being only a few hundred yards away.

Figure 26 Trail at "To Rockport" leads to the old mill site

Nearing the end of our trek, we have a choice of two paths, both of which end up on the Moraine Trail. To the right of Uncle Andrew's Rock, one leads through an old pasture and intersects the Moraine Trial below Colonial Pearce's cellar (C23). Going the other way takes us past a few more Boulders, and ends up a little closer to Dogtown Square between cellars 21 and 22.

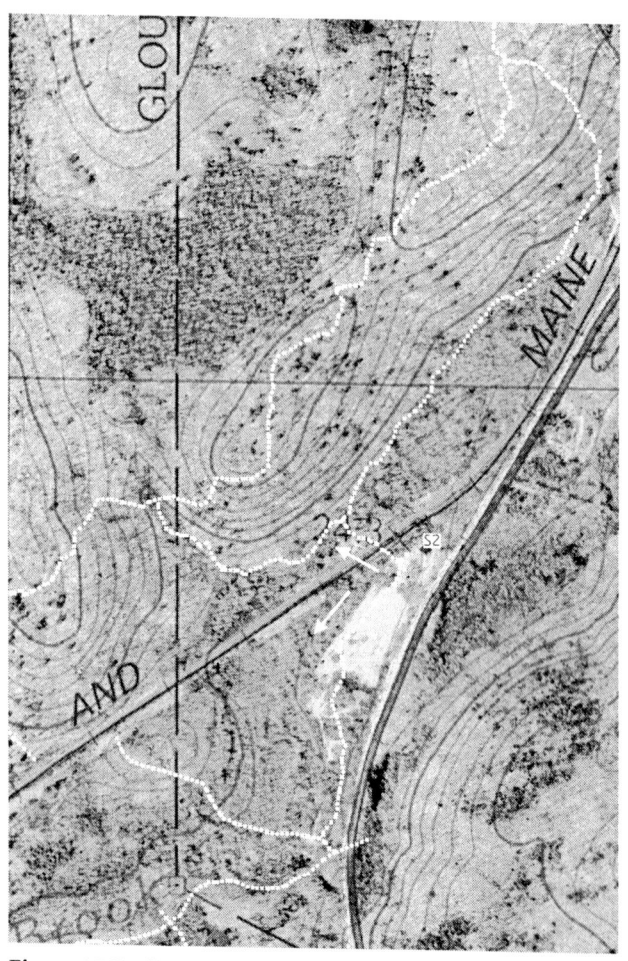

Figure 27 Trails behind Babson Shop on Eastern Avenue

Babson Shop

The Babson Shop (also called the Babson Museum) at Beaver Dam (S2) is another good place to enter Dogtown. Built in 1638, this building was James Babson's Cooperage Shop. In it he manufactured barrels that were used to ship dried fish to England. The barrels were made from wooden boards that were sawed downstream at the mill and transported by ox cart along Old Rockport Road to the road that runs past the stonewall in front of the shop (Figure 28).

A trail to Old Rockport Road (down arrow in Figure 27), which leads to the south side of Dogtown, runs through the field to our left. Behind the Babson Shop, a path (up arrow) takes us across the railroad tracks to a stone bridge over Alewife Brook[9] (Figure 29). On the other side is trail that offers two choices, both of which end up on the Tarr Trail at the top of the hill in front of us. Going to the right, we parallel a marsh. This can be a difficult trail to follow. At certain times of the year when the ground is wet and muddy, it is better to walk along the bottom of the hill to the left.

---

[9] Formerly known as Cape Pond Brook, Alewife Brook drains a large area of wetlands west of Cape Pond (located in Rockport's South Woods on the other side of Eastern Avenue). A waterway, which was once dug between Cape Pond and Cape Pond Brook, can be found to the right of the Babson Shop. Emerging from a culvert under Eastern Avenue, it flows under the old road that once ran past the shop, and into Alewife Brook.

After about a third of a mile, just past a stonewall, if one is not careful, it is easy to lose the trail in a field of boulders and fallen trees. If you can locate a stonewall that climbs up the hill on the left, the trail can be found just to the right of the wall. Continuing our hike up through rocks and trees, we eventually meet up with the Tarr Trail at marker #13 in a clearing on the top of the hill.

Figure 28 James Babson's shop on Eastern Avenue

An alternate route, which also leads to the Tarr Trail, is to go left on the path on the other side of the stone bridge, and follow it up along Wine Brook. Aside from finding a good place to cross the stream, this is a drier and a much easier trail to follow, meeting up with the Tarr Trail as it begins its ascent up the hill towards Dogtown.

Figure 29 Bridge behind the Babson Shop

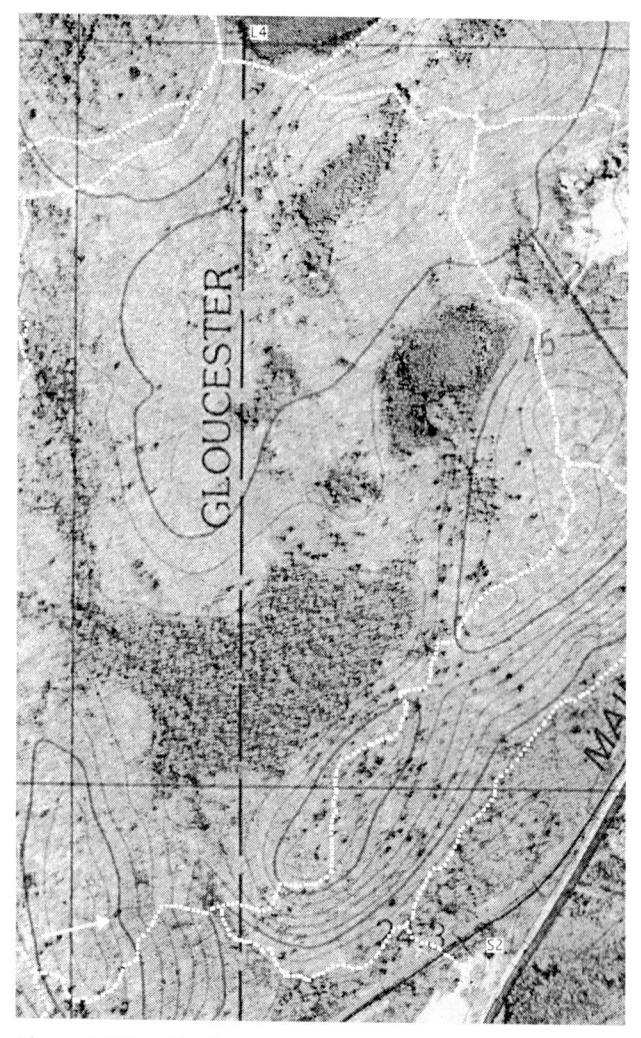

Figure 30 Tarr Trail northwest of Babson Shop

Tarr Trail

This trail is named after Ted Tarr, whose ancestors were among Rockport's early settlers. Beginning near a spring along the Moraine Trail (arrow in Figure 30), the Tarr Trail runs parallel to the terminal moraine through some of the roughest terrain in Dogtown. After a steep climb, we find ourselves on a granite terrace with several large boulders on which to rest. The trail then begins its descent to Wine Brook.

Figure 31 Wine Brook

Wine Brook, which drains an expanse of wetlands to the north, was originally named for the color of its water. Runoff stained by peat and bog iron deposits in Briar Swamp at one time flowed through these wetlands into Wine Brook. When the Babson Reservoir was constructed in the early 1930's, the south end of Briar Swamp was dammed to prevent the discolored water from flowing into Wine Brook.

Being the primary feed into Alewife Brook this in turn kept the water out of Babson Reservoir.

After crossing over Wine Brook, the climb up out of the other side of the valley is a bit steeper. Leveling off, the Tarr Trail heads northeast along a ridge. To the left is the stillness of the Great Swamp, and Briar Swamp beyond. To the right are the sounds of traffic on Eastern Avenue. After about two thirds of a mile, the Tarr Trail meets up with a secondary trail at marker #13, and continues on to its junction with the Luce Trail a third of a mile beyond.

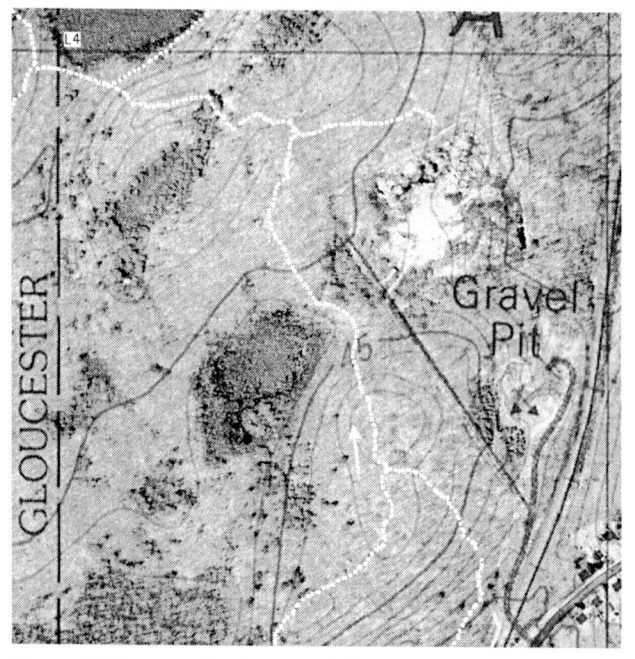

Figure 32 Start of the Luce Trail in Rockport

Luce Trail

The Luce[10] Trail starts at an opening in a stonewall north of the Gravel Pit in Rockport. This is not an easy place to get to, either on foot or by car. Instead, follow the Tarr Trail north from the Babson Shop as described in the previous section. Going left at the intersection (see arrow in Figure 32) with the Luce Trail takes us through the terminal moraine at Raccoon Ledges. On the other side of the boulder field, we meet up with the Rockport Town Forest Trail south of Briar Swamp.

The trail continues across a stone dam (Figure 33) at the south end of Briar Swamp. Look to the right for a path entering the swamp. Following this path leads us to the Boardwalk (L4), which cuts through the southwestern corner of Briar Swamp (Figure 34). Experts estimate that there are about 5,000 varieties of plants on Cape Ann. Many can be found in the Briar Swamp including the insectivorous Pitcher plant[11]. Exiting the swamp, we meet back up with the Luce Trail a short distance away near an unmarked cellar hole.

---

[10] Luce George lived on Fox Hill (south end of today's Cherry Street). Her niece was Tammy Younger. Both were thought to be witches. According to Charles E. Mann in his *Story of Dogtown*, they would stand at the door of her cabin and bewitch oxen until their drivers would pay a toll – a portion of whatever they were carrying.

[11] Further information about the flora and fauna of Cape Ann can be found in Eleanor Pope's *The Wilds of Cape Ann*, and in Helen Naismith's book, *Walking Cape Ann with Ted Tarr*.

Just past the dam, Art's and Nellie's Trails join up with the Luce Trail as we bear right and head north.

Figure 33 Stone barrier at the south end of Briar Swamp

Figure 34 Boardwalk through Briar Swamp

Continuing along the Luce Trail (arrow in Figure 35), we turn left at the intersection of a secondary trail (not shown in map). Now heading west, look for a stream off to the right that runs parallel to the trail. The stream is actually a waterway that was dug to

49

allow Briar Swamp to drain into the wetlands area north of Dogtown Commons. Up ahead we cross over it, just after turning right at the intersection of Common Road. Whale's Jaw (L1) is about two hundred yards up the hill to the left.

Leveling off, the trail zigzags along a ridge up to the north of the Briar Swamp where it meets up with Squam Path. There is a cellar hole at the junction. The two trails continue together as one past old cellar holes, foundation stones, and the Gloucester-Rockport town line. After another two hundred yards, Squam Path branches off to the left toward the Norton Farm. This was originally part of the "Road from Sandy Bay to Squam Meeting House through the Woods," which dates back to the 1700's. On the right is a trail that leads to Johnson's Quarry, one of the few granite quarries still in operation on Cape Ann. Continuing straight on leads north to Lanesville and Pigeon Cove.

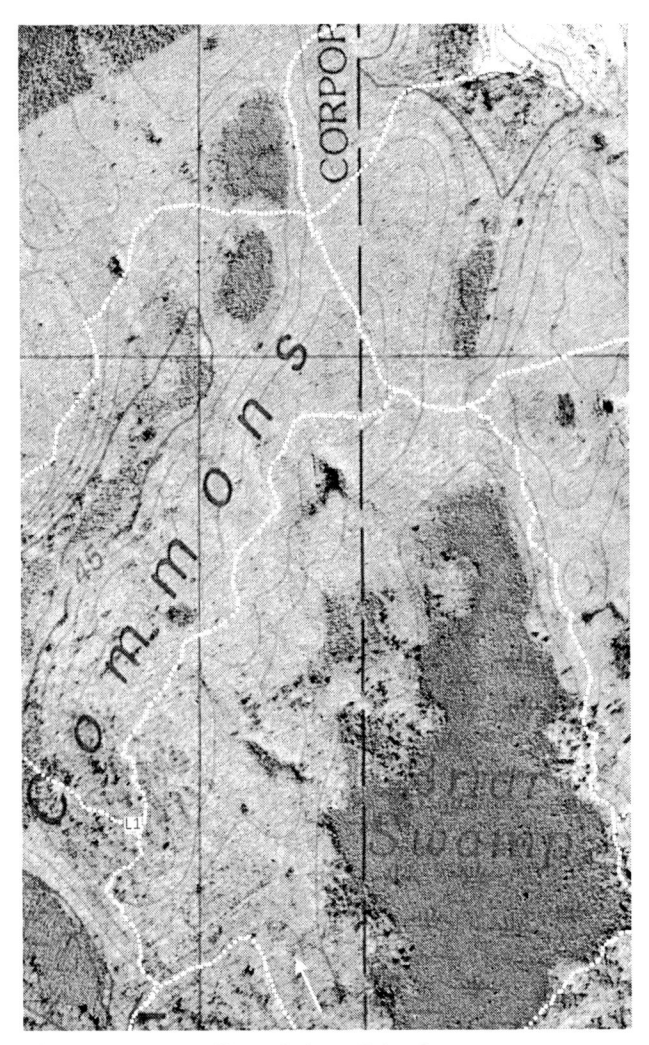

Figure 35 Luce Trail north from Briar Swamp

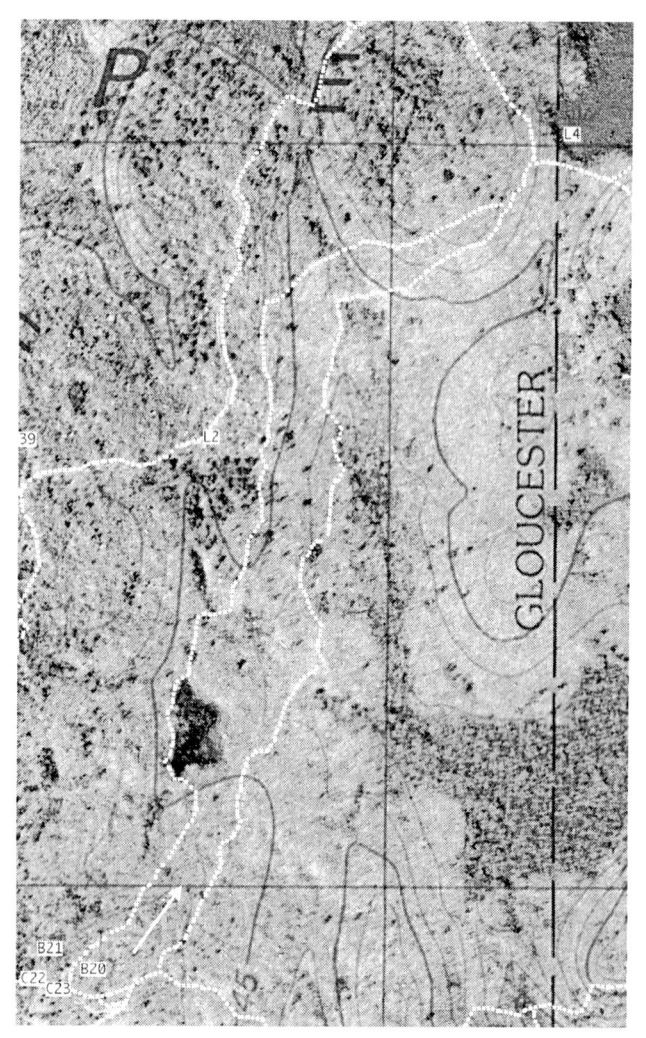

Figure 36 Art's and Nellie's trails

Art's and Nellie's Trails

Named for husband and wife conservationists, these two trails run from the Moraine Trail (in the direction of the arrow in Figure 36) to Briar Swamp. Although never more than a few hundred feet apart, they offer different perspectives of the terrain in the middle of Dogtown. From the *Dogtown Common Trail Map*,

"In general Nellie's takes the high road where new forest is emerging from long overgrown pasture, and Art's takes the low road near wooded swamps..."

Both trails start as well-defined paths through the woods, Nellie's, which is west of Art's, goes past one of Babson's rocks, "Prosperity Follows Service" (B20). A quarter mile in Art's Trail passes through a stonewall east of a vernal pond. Nellie's is across the pond just up the hill. Soon, both are lost in an enormous boulder field, with the only indication of a trail being one of Ted Tarr's colored paint dots on an occasional rock or tree. (Be careful not to confuse lichens, a kind of fungus that grows on trees and rocks, with paint dots.)

Two-thirds of the way along Nellie's Trail, one enters a grove of pines. Looking to the left, one spots a giant rock through the trees. A short detour takes us through the woods to Peter's Pulpit (L2) a couple of hundred feet away. Continuing on, Art's and Nellie's Trails wind around the upper end of a vast wetlands area. Just before reaching Briar Swamp, they level off and become one, intersecting the Luce Trail west of the stone dike at Briar Swamp.

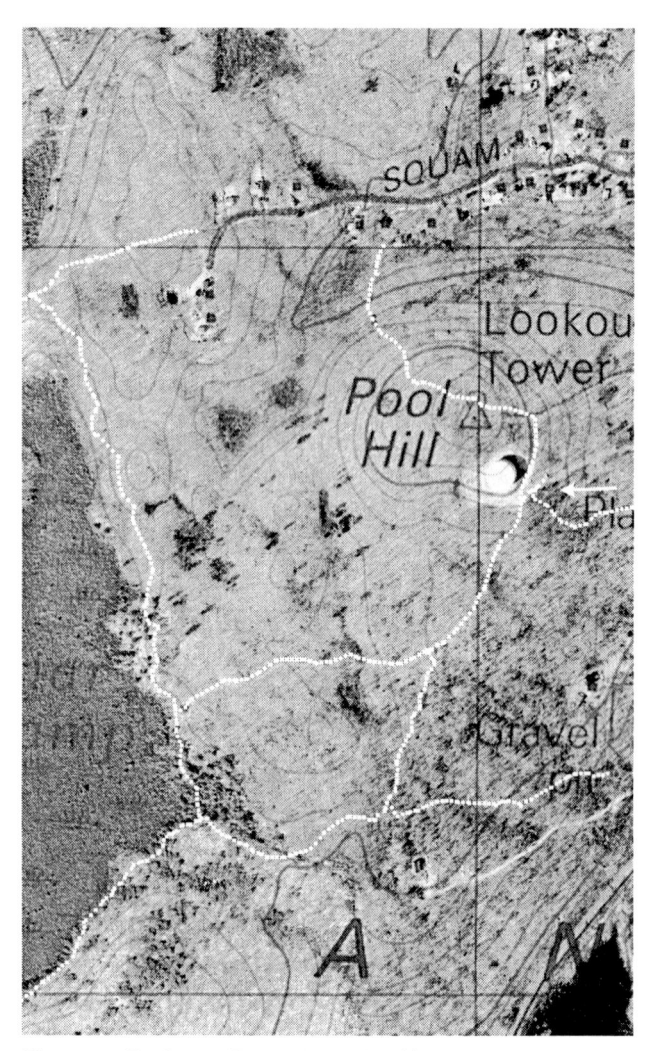

Figure 37 Rockport Town Forest Trail

Rockport Town Forest Trail

This trail is a good way to enter Dogtown from the Town of Rockport. After parking at the Rockport Train Station, walk into Evans Field, and look for stone steps going up the hill in front of us. The steps lead to a trail up to the water tank at the end of Summit Avenue. We have two choices (at the arrow in Figure 37). Continuing across to the right is a fire road that goes up to Squam Road. There are several unmarked cellar holes along this route.

The other option is to go left and follow the Rockport Town Forest Trail to Briar Swamp. About a quarter of a mile in, at a large cellar hole, a secondary trail splits off to the left that takes a more southerly (and wetter) route to the swamp. Though laurel and hemlock, this trail passes back and forth over a stream, crossing an old stone bridge at one point.

If instead we stay on the main road, after another quarter of a mile it suddenly ends. Not to panic. Walking twenty paces further we find ourselves on a north-south trail, which runs along the east side of Briar Swamp. Going left on this trail, we eventually meet up with the secondary trail mentioned above. If you do take the secondary trail, stay on it until you reach Briar Swamp. Several smaller paths that branch off before the swamp stray to the east and lead to the Gravel Pit north of Loop Pond. Just before reaching the southern end of Briar Swamp, the Rockport Town Forest Trail merges with the Luce Trail.

If instead one wishes to go the other way, take a right at the end of the Town Forest Trail. Heading north the trail winds up a hill and follows the high ground east of Briar Swamp, meeting up with Squam Path less than a half a mile away.

Figure 38 Fire road in the Rockport Town Forest

Another good way to enter Dogtown from the Rockport side is to walk up Squam Road from Granite Street. Near the end of the road, there is a gate that blocks vehicular traffic. This is the Squam Path, which in Mason's 1831 map of Gloucester is a part of the "Road from Sandy Bay to Squam Meeting House through the Woods." That road ran across the Cape from what is today's Revere Street to Squam Road (Figure 39).

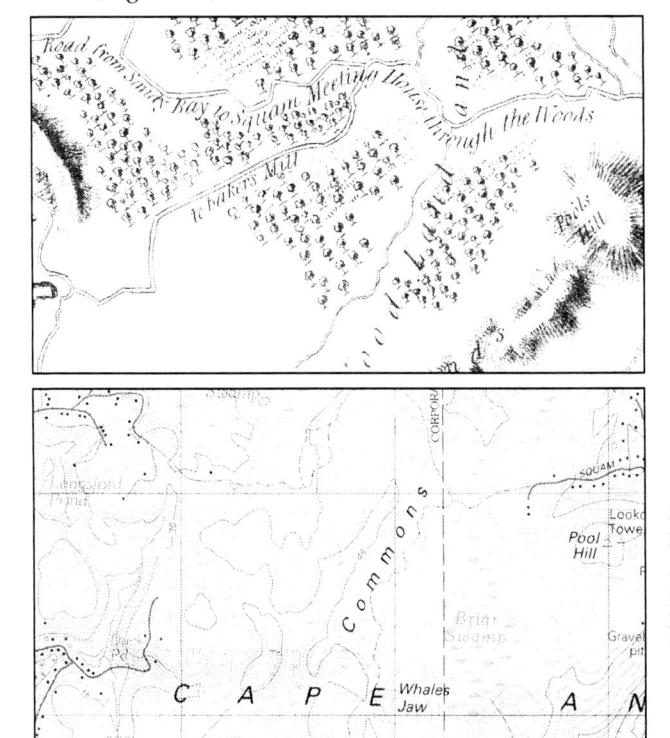

Figure 39 Squam Path in portion of Mason's map (top) and USGS topographic map (bottom)

Figure 40 Stonewall leading east into the interior of the Commons from Goose Cove Reservoir

Interior of the Commons

Although much of Dogtown was once open land, dense vegetation limits access to sites along roads and trails. Following stonewalls provides a way to get to more remote areas in Dogtown. One example is site S, located north of what was the Commons Pasture (Figure 41). A house was built there by Nehemiah Stanwood, and later occupied by Peter Lurvey, and others through the early 19th century.

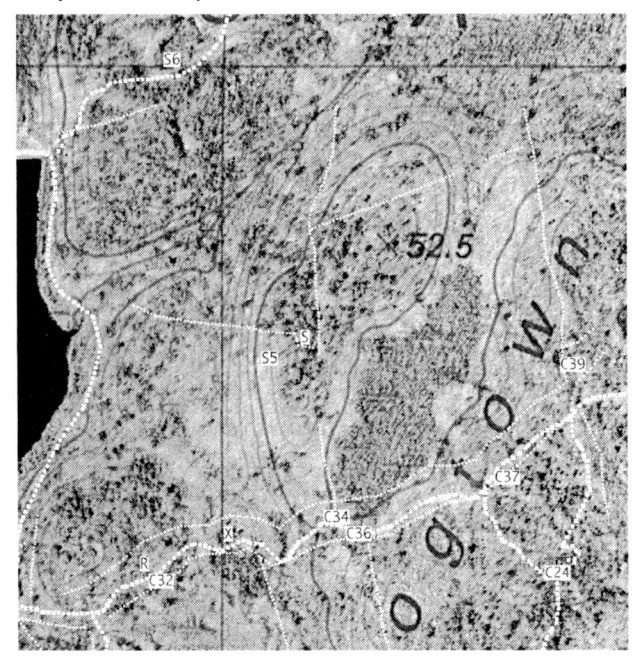

Figure 41 Stonewalls in Dogtown

As one walks along the service road on the east side of Goose Cove Reservoir, a number of stonewalls can be seen in the woods. Just past the brook, a wall runs up the hill and off into the woods on the left[12]. Follow the wall about a quarter of mile east, through a marshy area, and up the hill (Figure 40).

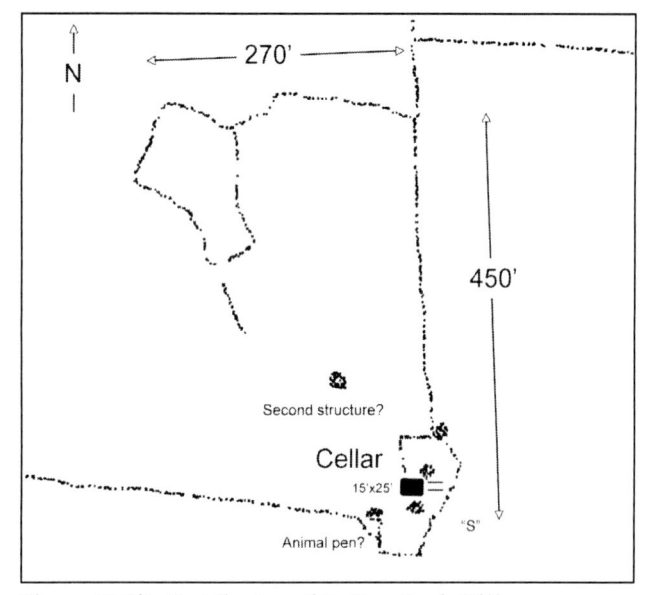

Figure 42 Site S at the top of Rotten Rock Hill

---

[12] Walking through the woods in winter offers the best view of these walls as they recede into the distance. With minimal vegetation, and no insects, this is also the best time to hike through the brush. Still, briars can make passage difficult in places, and may result in a few scratches.

The site is at the top of the hill, to the left of the wall. A boulder that Babson inscribed with the letter "S" is just east of the site. According to Mann, a number of people lived here, but it is not clear if they lived in the same house, or if there were multiple dwellings. The site is rather large, about 2 acres in size (Figure 42). The actual cellar is at the southeast corner. It is about 15x25 feet in area and at least 5 feet deep. The cellar stones are large and more or less intact (Figure 43). There is evidence of a second structure a short distance away to the northwest.

Figure 43 Lurvey Cellar (S)

One curious feature at the corner of a stonewall southwest of the Lurvey cellar is a semi-circular area enclosed with rocks that might have been an animal pen. Another feature just like this one can be found about a quarter mile to the east, at the junction of two other stonewalls.

Figure 44 Wall of quarried stone in the middle of the Commons

Instead of backtracking one can bushwhack south down to Common Road. On the way a large wall made of quarried stone (S5) can be seen along the side of a hill (Figure 44). The structure, which post dates the original settlement, might have been the foundation of a barn used by animals grazing on the Beech Pasture in Dogtown's later years.

The stonewall we followed in from Goose Cove Reservoir continues on for a considerable distance. It descends into a marsh, ascends, and intersects a stonewall on the other side of the Commons Pasture. A better way to visit this side of Dogtown is to take Common Road to Benjamin Allen's cellar (C39). Follow the stonewall on the north side of the road as it enters the brush just before the site. About two hundred yards north, there is a gap in the wall that might have been an old trail crossing. Farther on, the continuation of the wall in from Goose Cove Reservoir intersects from the left. There is a circular arrangement of stones here just like those mentioned earlier at site S that resemble an animal pen. Although there is no record of a house having been built in this part of Dogtown, one wonders if there was something, perhaps a small barn, here.

Figure 45 Pattern of circular stones that might have served as an animal pen

Appendix

Geographic Coordinates of Cellar Holes and Other Sites in Dogtown

ID	Cellar/Site	Latitude	Longitude
C12	Wilson	42.63664	-70.66090
C13	Winslow	42.63716	-70.66024
C14	H. Stephens	42.63758	-70.65959
C16	Dermerit	42.63851	-70.65614
C17	Foster	42.63891	-70.65638
C18	Dade	42.63908	-70.65596
C19	Ingersoll	42.63917	-70.65527
C20	Day (School)	42.63975	-70.65477
C20A	Day	42.64035	-70.65342
C21	Robinson	42.63966	-70.65287
C22	Riggs	42.63943	-70.65217
C23	Pearce	42.63931	-70.65174
C24	A. Wharf	42.64346	-70.65276
C28	Bennet	42.64175	-70.66585
C29	Hilton	42.64191	-70.66501
C30	Hunter & Elwell	42.64387	-70.65841
C31	White	42.64229	-70.66097
C32	Davis	42.64329	-70.65957
C34	March	42.64409	-70.65655
C36	Whipple	42.64390	-70.65617

C37	Wither	42.64462	-70.65365
C39	Allen	42.64600	-70.65255
C9	Clark	42.63590	-70.66179
N	M. Stephens	42.63740	-70.65885
R	Rhines	42.64339	-70.65977
S	Stanwood/Lurvey	42.64628	-70.65713
X	Elwell	42.64387	-70.65841
S1	First Mill	42.63237	-70.64978
S2	Babson Shop	42.63882	-70.63887
S3	School house	42.63166	-70.64903
S4	Foundation	42.64214	-70.65870
S5	Wall	42.64602	-70.65773
S6	Fireplace	42.64963	-70.65949
S7	Quarry	42.63025	-70.65522

ID	Feature	Latitude	Longitude
L1	Whale's Jaw	42.65308	-70.64755
L2	Peter's Pulpit	42.64608	-70.64935
L3	Overlook	42.64127	-70.66130
L4	Boardwalk	42.64987	-70.64326

Roger Babson

It is almost certain that the center of Cape Ann and Dogtown would not be as they are today were it not for Roger Babson. Born in 1875, he was the tenth generation of his family to live in Gloucester. After attending the Massachusetts Institute of Technology, Babson worked at several investment firms before establishing the Babson Institute (now Babson College) in 1919.

A successful entrepreneur and business theorist, Babson's passion was Cape Ann and Dogtown. During the Great Depression he hired unemployed stone workers from the Cape's granite quarries to carve inscriptions in boulders on family-owned land. This land was later donated to the City of Gloucester, and forms the watershed for the reservoir created in the 1930s and named in his honor.

The table below lists the geographic coordinates of the Babson Boulders.

ID	Quote	Latitude	Longitude
B1	Get a Job	42.62885	-70.65625
B2	Help Mother	42.62912	-70.65641
B3	Be True	42.62920	-70.65557
B4	Be Clean	42.62942	-70.65608
B5	Save	42.62946	-70.65652
B6	Truth	42.63191	-70.65520
B7	Work	42.63214	-70.65466
B8	Courage	42.63270	-70.65328

B9	To Rockport	42.63315	-70.65287
B10	Loyalty	42.63458	-70.65281
B11	Kindness	42.63630	-70.65333
B12	Intelligence	42.63726	-70.65331
B13	Ideals	42.63739	-70.65262
B14	Ideas	42.63753	-70.65304
B15	Integrity	42.63774	-70.65285
B16	Initiative	42.63787	-70.65305
B17	Industry	42.63798	-70.65268
B18	Spiritual Power	42.63798	-70.65242
B19	Be On Time/Study	42.63872	-70.65257
B20	Prosperity Follows Service	42.63956	-70.65114
B21	If Work Stops Values Decay	42.63980	-70.65189
B22	Keep Out of Debt	42.64014	-70.65286
B23	Moraine	42.64005	-70.65334
B24	D.T. SQ	42.64018	-70.65376
B25	Never Try Never Win	42.63888	-70.65532
B26	Use Your Head	42.63862	-70.65229

Bibliography

Elizabeth Waugh, *The First People of Cape Ann*, Dogtown Books, Gloucester MA, 2005.

Joseph E. Garland, *The Gloucester Guide*, The History Press, Charleston SC, 2004.

The Dogtown Mural-Map, The Pressroom, Gloucester MA, 1999.

Thomas Dresser, *Dogtown: A Village Lost in Time*, Thorn Books, Franconia NH, 1995.

Gloucester, Massachusetts, Maps Showing Early Gloucester, Archives Committee, City of Gloucester, MA, 1995.

Helen Naismith, *Walking Cape Ann with Ted Tarr*, Ten Pound Island Books, Gloucester MA, 1994.

Irving Sucholeiki, *A Return to Dogtown: A Look at the Artifacts Left Behind by Some of Cape Ann's Early Settlers*, Chisholm and Hunt Printers, Inc. Gloucester MA, 1992.

Dogtown Common Trail Map, The Pressroom, Gloucester MA, 1987.

Developing a Management Program for Dogtown: A Report to the Mayor by the Dogtown Steering Committee, Gloucester MA, 1985.

Christine Leigh Heyrman, *Commerce and Culture: The Maritime Communities of Colonial Massachusetts 1690-1750*, W.W. Norton & Company, New York, 1984.

Eleanor Pope, *The Wilds of Cape Ann*, Nimrod Press, Boston MA, 1981.

The Saga of Cape Ann, M. Copeland and E. Rogers, Bond Wheelwright Company, Freeport ME, 1960.

W. H. Dennen, *The Rocks of Cape Ann*, The Gloucester Cultural Commission.

Roger W. Babson and Foster H. Saville, *Cape Ann Tourist's Guide*, Sandy Bay Historical Society and Museum Inc., Rockport MA, 1936.

Along the Old Roads of Cape Ann, Cape Ann Scientific and Literary Society, 1923.

Charles E. Mann, *In the Heart of Cape Ann or the Story of Dogtown*, Proctor Bros. Publishers, Gloucester MA, 1896.

James R. Pringle, *History of the Town and City of Gloucester, Cape Ann, Massachusetts*, Gloucester MA, 1892.

John J. Babson, *History of the Town of Gloucester, Cape Ann*, Proctor Bros., Gloucester, MA, 1860.

Map of Gloucester and Cape Ann, John Mason (1831), Ten Pound Island Books.

Index

Adams Pines, 13, 18, 19, 20, 24

Adams, Rayne, 19

Alewife Brook, 31, 33, 34, 41, 46

Allen, Benjamin, 14, 27, 62

animal pen, 61, 63

Annisquam River, 3

Art's Trail, 29, 48, 52, 53

Babson Boulder Trail, 28, 31, 35, 36, 37, 38

Babson Boulders, 3, 4, 37, 69

Babson Reservoir, 3, 23, 31, 34, 37, 45, 46

Babson Shop, 3, 30, 33, 40, 41, 43, 44, 47

Babson, James, 32, 41, 42

Babson, Roger W., 9, 10, 13, 19, 23, 24, 27, 28, 32, 33, 34, 53, 61, 69, 72

barn, 62, 63

Beaver Dam, 4, 30, 41

Beech Pasture, 14, 62

Bennett, Anthony, 10, 11

Blackburn Industrial Park, 3, 31

blacksmith, 14

Boardwalk, 47, 49, 68

Briar Swamp, 4, 29, 45, 46, 47, 48, 49, 50, 51, 53, 55, 56

brook, 8, 9, 10, 15, 19, 32, 34, 60

Cape Ann, 1, 2, 4, 5, 19, 31, 47, 69, 71, 72

Cape Pond, 33, 41

Captain Kidd, 13

Carter, Easter, 23

Castle, 11

cellar holes, 1, 3, 4, 21, 24, 28, 33, 50, 55

Cherry Street, 3, 23

cobbler, 9

73

Common Road, 9, 12, 13, 14, 15, 16, 19, 27, 50, 62

common woodlands, 7

Commons Settlement, 1, 7, 15, 25, 31

Copeland, Melvin T. and Rogers, Elliott C., 27

dam, 7, 10, 17, 18, 34, 47, 48

Day, Jane "Granny", 22, 25, 27, 67

Dennison Street, 2, 7, 17, 18

Dogtown Commons, 3, 4, 23, 50

Dogtown Road, 3, 10, 19, 21, 22, 23, 24, 25, 37

Dogtown Square, 27, 39

Eastern Avenue, 3, 33, 40, 42, 46

Elwell, Joshua, 9

erratic, 14, 15

farm, 11, 20, 21, 23, 27, 28

Finson, Cornelius, 13

foundation, 7, 17, 18, 19, 50, 62

gate, 3, 7, 10, 23, 57

Gee Avenue, 3, 7, 9, 11, 13

George, Luce, 47

glaciers, 15

global positioning system, 4

Gloucester, 1, 3, 7, 19, 25, 28, 31, 33, 35, 38, 50, 57, 69, 71, 72

Goose Cove Reservoir, 2, 3, 6, 7, 10, 11, 13, 17, 21, 23, 58, 60, 62

Granite Street, 56

Granny Day's Swamp, 27

gravel pit, 47, 55

heath, 21

Hilton, William, 9

Hunter, Joshua, 9

Ipswich Bay, 10, 21, 37

Johnson's Quarry, 50

Lanesville, 2, 17, 50

lichens, 53

Luce Trail, 15, 17, 46, 47, 48, 49, 51, 53, 55

Lurvey, Peter, 13, 59, 61, 68

Mann, Charles E., 13, 27, 47, 61, 72

Mason, John, 31, 57, 72

meadow, 10, 33

Meeting House, 31, 50, 57

Meeting House Green, 31

Merry, James, 24, 25

mill, 31, 32, 33, 34, 35, 38, 39, 41, 68

Mill River, 15, 34

moraine, 29, 45, 47

Moraine Trail, 26, 27, 28, 29, 33, 39, 45, 53

Nellie's Trail, 29, 48, 52, 53

Old Gravel Road, 23, 37

Old Rockport Road, 2, 3, 30, 31, 32, 33, 35, 37, 38, 41

Olson, Charles, 24

pastureland, 15

Pearce, Col. William, 28, 29, 39, 67

Peter's Pulpit, 13, 14, 15, 37, 53

quarried stone, 19, 62

quarry, 31

railroad tracks, 30, 31, 33, 35, 37, 41

Revere Street, 57

Rhines, Judy, 13

Riverdale, 34

Robinson, James, 27

Rockport, 2, 3, 4, 31, 45, 46, 47, 50, 55, 56

Rockport Town Forest Trail, 4, 47, 54, 55

scenic overlook, 10

schoolhouse, 25, 32

Spiritual Power, 28, 38, 70

Squam Path, 4, 17, 50, 56, 57

Squam Road, 2, 55, 56

Stannard, Granther, 9

Stanwood, John Morgan, 9

Stanwood, Nehemiah, 13, 59

stone bridge, 13, 41, 43, 55

stonewalls, 1, 7, 10, 13, 20, 37, 59, 60, 61

stream, 13, 17, 37, 43, 49, 55

Sucholeiki, Irving, 27, 71

Tarr Trail, 29, 41, 43, 44, 45, 46, 47

Tarr, Ted, 45, 47, 53, 71

trail marker, 29, 42, 46

Tucker, Liz, 13

Uncle Andrew's Rock, 28, 37, 38, 39

vernal pond, 21, 38

wall, 10, 62, 68

Washington Street, 3, 13

waterway, 41, 49

well, 27, 29

wetlands, 8, 17, 19, 45, 50, 53

Whale's Jaw, 7, 13, 15, 17, 50

Wharf Road, 14, 26, 27

Wharf, Abraham, 27

Wine Brook, 43, 45, 46

Winslow, Joseph, 21, 23, 67

witches, 47

Witham, James, 27

Younger, Tammy, 47

Notes